WINNING THE WAR
AGAINST
MARRIAGE KILLERS

Ladejola Abiodun

TABLE OF CONTENTS

Introduction 9

Chapter 1: 11

Chapter 2: 23

Chapter 3: 37

Chapter 4: 45

Chapter 5: 59

Chapter 6: 73

Conclusion 85

Bonus Section: Prophetic Declarations & Decrees 93

Deliverance from foundational bondages and yokes .. 95

Breaking the hold of family idol and ancestral strongman 103

Breaking evil soul tie 109

Destroy satanic remote controlling power working against your life.............. 113

Destroy satanic covenant that hinders progress........ 117

Ejecting of poison of darkness from your body.......... 121

Deliverance from the shadow of death 125

Pulling down satanic stronghold militating against you 129

A cry of solution to difficult problems 135

Deliverance from stubborn foundational bondage ... 139

Breaking the backbone of domestic witchcraft.......... 143

Deliverance from evil family altars 147

Deliverance from the grip of house hold wickedness. 151

Breaking the yoke of familiar spirits and Marine spirits 155

Deliverance from bondage of polygamy 159

Deliverance from placental bondage........................ 163

Violent prayers against unrepentant household wickedness and pursuers... 167

Prayers to destroy oppression and bondage 173

Prayers of deliverance from limitation and stagnation 179

Books By Pastor Ladejola Abiodun 185

DEDICATION

This book is dedicated to God Almighty, the giver of all knowledge and our Saviour, the Lord Jesus Christ.

INTRODUCTION

Marriage is God's idea, not man's. When it works, it is the most beautiful thing to behold. However, there are **powers assigned** to make sure it doesn't work for many families on earth. **Marriage killers** are these powers. They are **enemies of holy unions.**

They are the **powers and principalities** directed by the demonic kingdom to attack good marriages and Christian homes. They manifest themselves in a vast array of ways.

Their endgame is to cause **divorce, emotional distress**, the **derailment of destinies** of children born into this world, **death**, and **eternal damnation**. This powerful book exposes the strategies of these marriage killers and how to defeat them. God bless you.

Ladejola Abiodun

CHAPTER 1:

THE WAR AGAINST MARRIAGE KILLERS

Marriage is God's idea, not man's. The Bible says when God created man, He also created animals like hippopotamuses, lions, goats, monkeys, etc. However, all these animals were in pairs, only man was alone. Then God said, "It is not good that the man should be alone" (Gen. 2:18). This is the foundation of the marriage institution by God.

Godly Instructions for Godly Marriage

As God is the Founder of the first institution (marriage), the instructions to run it must also come from Him, just as every manufacturer attaches an instruction manual to any product that has been made. It is this manual that specifies how to use and maximize the utility of the product. Similarly, instructions on how a marriage should go must come from God, and not from Harvard, not from Oxford, or music celebrities. It is not what men can reason or fathom: *the word of God, the Bible,* is the working manual of the marriage institution.

As far as marriage is concerned, the first instruction you find in the Bible with reference to marriage is found in Genesis 2:24:

"Therefore shall a man leave his father and his mother, and shall cleave unto his wife: and they shall be one flesh."

This is not a suggestion, nor an opinion. It is God's conclusive instruction and it states that a married man should leave his father and mother and cleave unto his wife, and they shall be one flesh or one entity.

Marriage is also designed by God for glory and honor. It is not designed for shame or dishonor. God created the marriage institution to make a man better, not to make him worse. Marriage is for fruitfulness and blessing, and not for poverty or ridicule.

In Psalm 68:6, the Bible says, *"God setteth the solitary in families..."* The word 'solitary' means loneliness. Therefore, God's own way of curing loneliness is marriage. God's method of eliminating loneliness in a man's life is marriage. Marriage does not take from a man or a woman; it adds to him or her. It completes and complements them; it makes a man or a woman better. That is why the Bible says, *"Two are better than one; because they have a good reward for their labour. For if they fall, the one will lift up his fellow: but woe to him that is alone when he falleth; for he hath not another to help him up"* (Eccl. 4:9-10).

A marriage that is in the will of God attracts favour from God and man. When you pattern your marriage after God's heart and God's will, you will become a candidate of favour. Proverbs 18:22 says, "Whosoever findeth a wife findeth a good thing, and obtaineth favour of the Lord."

Marriage as a Holy Wedlock

Marriage is a holy wedlock, and not bad luck. This means it is designed for pleasure and not for pain. It is designed for joy and not for sorrow; it is designed to be enjoyed and not to be endured. Neither the wife nor the husband is complete without the other; nobody is complete in himself or herself.

Because marriage is a holy wedlock, it involves serious commitment. It involves 'leaving and cleaving', and this is where a lot of people are missing it. The commitment involved in marriage is very high. To make a marriage work is a combination of effort: it must not be one person only servicing the marriage. It must be a joint effort. All the parties (the man and the woman) must come together and contribute their quota. Every party must play his or her roles very well. It is a serious commitment and when the parties are committed, good and tangible results will soon show.

Unfortunately, many people are just excited about marriage, they do not know or honour the commitment that goes with it.

Creativity is needed in Your Marriage

Another thing you need to know is that in the institution of marriage, you have to be very creative because if you are not, everything will soon become boring. If you are not creative, the excitement you used to feel about your partner will die off. As a result of this, you must keep on 'servicing' your marriage and finding innovative ways to bring it to life.

Creativity means not to be boring, but to be lively. You may feel some of those romantic things that you were doing in those days for your spouse are old and archaic, and you drop them because you feel you are growing old, but it is not so in marriage. To enjoy your marriage, you must keep doing those 'old' romantic things, like touching your partner or holding her hands. No man or woman of any age can outgrow that. They should not take the other person for granted. A husband and wife need to spend time together: to play together, to pray together and to do things together.

Marriage Involves Leaving and Cleaving

Marriage involves leaving and cleaving. I choose to emphasize this because it is very important. If you are privileged to come into our counseling rooms, you will hear the stories of many men that are still tied to their parents' apron strings. I have seen situations where it is the mother that is deciding for the man. It is the mother that decides what happens in the family. It is the same mother that gives instructions on what should be done. If you cannot leave and cleave, you are not matured enough for marriage. Until you can cleave and settle down to run your home, you will not enjoy God's divine favour and blessing in marriage.

As a woman, if any little thing the man does makes you to pack your load and say, "I'm going", you will soon have a permanent apartment in your father's house.

There are many people who are married today; people see them as been married, but they are separated, because there is a division between them as a couple. They do not do things together as a couple. The husband goes this way while the wife goes the other way. Unfortunately, this has also divided the children. There are couples who abuse each other in front of the children.

For instance, the man will verbally abuse the wife in front of the children, saying something like, "See, your mother is a useless woman, she is a shameless woman". Then, the woman too will corner the children and say: "Your father is a lazy man, he is not fit to be a man, and on top of that, he is a poor man!"

Many men also use their **financial power** to draw their children to themselves against their wives. Let me say this; anything you do to your wife, your children are watching you. There is a soft spot in the children's heart towards their mother. If a man hates his wife, who is his children's mother, although the children have no choice now, they will pay him back in the future when they have grown and remember what he did. They will think of what the woman went through to bring them to life. Because they know that it is the man that is paying their school fees now, they may pretend not to care but when the time comes, they will show him.

Some men have done everything to **destroy the image of their wives** before their children. The children will follow him sheepishly but he will not know that they are just waiting for their time of deliverance. When the time comes, the man will see that the greatest thing he can do before his children is to show to them that he **loves their mother**, and he must do everything possible to show to them that he loves the woman.

One boy told his father: "Daddy, I can see that every effort you are making in this house is to make me hate my mother. I observe that you like your own mother, but you want me to hate my own mother. No way!" All these can lead to **separation and divorce** which are not in the will of God for married couple.

WINNING THE WAR AGAINST MARRIAGE KILLERS

Divorce is Not an Option in Marriage

Marriage is designed for life. Divorce was not part of the original plan of God. The question is, where did divorce, separation and putting away come from, if they didn't come from God? Divorce is part of the **devil's agendas** against godly marriages.

At a time, the Pharisees went to Jesus and ask him some questions concerning marriage and the issue of divorce (Matt. 19:26). Jesus told them that from the beginning, the One who created marriage (God) did not factor divorce or separation into marriage. They asked him why Moses asked them to give a letter of divorce and allow the woman to go. He replied that the instruction did not come from God, but that Moses, because of the hardness of their hearts, allowed them to do so. He said it is the doctrine of Moses and not the commandment of God; it is Moses who devised this because he saw that their hearts were **hardened**. He said it was Moses who introduced this law because they were **stubborn and selfish**. Because of their unwillingness to change, their inability to forgive and let go, Moses decided to give this law. He said Moses **introduced this doctrine** because of their lack of wisdom. Jesus Christ himself said, '*What therefore God has joined together, let not man put asunder*' (Matt.19:6).

It is important to note that every marriage that breaks down is due to **lack of wisdom**. This is because the Bible says by wisdom is a house built and established (Prov.24:3). This means that it is through wisdom that a man or woman build and grow in marriage.

It takes **wisdom** for a marriage to grow from grace to grace and from glory to glory. Every broken marriage is a sign that wisdom is deficient. Do you know why? Solomon, a man that was reputed to be very wise has 700 wives and 300 concubines, and the man still performed his role as a king and husband. He uses his wisdom to manage all his wives. The man married 700 women and he still lived as a normal person.

If you have only one wife and at the age of 35, and you are having high blood pressure, you cannot sleep in your house and you are running from the house of a friend to another friend, it means you **lack wisdom**.

You need to realize that it takes **wisdom to marry** and to remain married. For you to be successful in the institution of marriage therefore, you need to understand that marriage is a **holy institution established by God**, know **God's purpose and instruction** concerning marriage, be **creative** to maintain and sustain the flame of love in your marriage, **cleave and be permanently bound** to your spouse, **obliterate all thoughts of divorce** from your mind, and **pray to God for wisdom** to fulfill His will and purpose for your marriage. It is by doing these that you will be able to successfully wage war against the marriage killers that threaten your marital sanctity.

Prayer Points

I prophesy **marital favour, blessing, goodness, and prosperity** into my marriage, in the name of Jesus.

I receive **wisdom to build my home** today, in the name of Jesus.

The **spirit of marriage destruction** will not succeed over my marriage, in the name of Jesus.

Through the **blood of Jesus**, I am redeemed from the grip of marriage killers, in the name of Jesus.

All **demonic manipulations** against my marital destiny, be frustrated now, in the name of Jesus.

God of Elijah, give me the **power to destroy all marriage killers** troubling my life, in the name of Jesus.

Spirit of the living God, overshadow my marriage, in the name of Jesus.

CHAPTER 2:

WHAT ARE MARRIAGE KILLERS?

Marriage killers are the enemies of marriage. They are the powers and principalities directed by the demonic kingdom to destroy good marriages and Christian homes. These marriage killers have access to the homes and marriages of prayerless Christians who do not follow God's instructions regarding the institution of marriage. Some of these marriage killers and how to handle them are highlighted below:

The spirit of marriage destruction

There is a spirit called the spirit of marriage destruction. If you come to the counseling room, you will hear a lot about the activities of this spirit.

Sometimes when you hear that a marriage is broken and you try to find out what caused this, you may discover that it is something that is so insignificant, or something that should have been overlooked by the couple, but it is this insignificant thing that wrecked the home. It is called the spirit of marriage destruction. This is what Solomon the wise man called the little fox that destroys the vineyard.

Song of Solomon 2:15 "Take us the foxes, the little foxes, that spoil the vines: for our vines have tender grapes."

This spirit has scattered the peace of many homes. It has attacked many homes, and separated many husbands and wives.

The spirit of division

This is the power which makes the wife go into the kitchen to cook her food, and when she finished, the husband will go there to cook his own; they sleep on the same bed but there is a giant pillow between them and their bodies do not touch. This is a very bad spirit and married couples should be united and join forces in prayer to wage war against this marriage killer.

The spirit of pride

This is holding on to your position or perspective, and vowing not to change. It is a spirit which says, "I am always right!". I have seen marriages that suffered for many years, just because the person who is at fault could not say 'sorry'. There was no peace in the home just because one person refused to say 'I'm sorry', and this destroyed the home.

The spirit of pride is manifested in a person stubbornly holding on to his or her stand, saying, 'I am the one that is right'. But the question is: what trophy are you going to collect for being right?

The activities of incubus and succubus.

Open your Bible to Jude 1:6-8:

"And the angels which kept not their first estate, but left their own habitation, he hath reserved in everlasting chains under darkness unto the judgment of the great day. Even as Sodom and Gomorrah, and the cities about them in like manner, giving themselves over to fornication, and going after strange flesh, are set forth for an example, suffering the vengeance of eternal fire. Likewise these filthy dreamers defile the flesh, despise dominion, and speak evil of dignities."

These are the spirits that come to trouble people in their dreams. The Bible calls them 'filthy dreamers' (Jude 8). They are also known as spirit spouses (spirit wives and husbands). Many marriages are going through a tough time today because of the activities of these spirit entities. They use sex in the dream to pollute and defile the human body, which is the temple of God. They use this ungodly sex in the dream to serve the purpose of Satan in a person's life.

Seeing yourself breastfeeding a child in the dream is satanic. It is demonic and through that, an individual is manipulated and the home is destroyed. This can manifest in forms of miscarriages, blocked wombs, impotence, fibroids, diseases of the internal organs, and all manner of spiritual attacks.

It is worse when the person does not see them. When you sleep and you don't know what happened during the hours of your sleep, and you can't remember your dreams; when you are not married but you see yourself getting married to a stranger in your dreams; when you are not pregnant but you are seeing milk or whitish substance like that of a pregnant woman coming out from your breasts, et cetera. All these are the activities of spirit spouses, and they use them to plant fibroids and other diseases in the victim's womb and internal organs.

The spirit of anger

Anger is a great enemy that troubles marriage. This spirit is not just a mere enemy, it is a virulent enemy that has destroyed many marriages. This avowed killer has sent many marriages to an early grave. It is this spirit that opens marriages up for demonic invasion and satanic occupation. It is a spirit that has brought heartache, tears, pains, and sorrow to many homes.

Anger is an emotion of displeasure which occurs when you feel offended. Sometimes, it is an uncontrolled emotion, and it has destroyed many homes beyond repair. Anger has aborted many marriages. The Bible says in Ecclesiastes 7:9 that anger rests in the bosom of fools. This means if there is anger in a person's life, there will be no value in that life: the person's life will become worthless and the person will become useless. That is why some people you hold in high honour and esteem become worthless on the day you see them get angry, and from that day the value you have for them drops. This happens when you see them throw a fit and refuse to be controlled.

An angry man or an angry woman is a potential murderer. The Bible records some cases where murder took place that were caused by the spirit of anger. Cain killed his brother Abel in anger. Simeon and Levi killed the Shechemites in anger. Moses killed an Egyptian because he was angry. Joab killed Abner and Amasa in a vengeful rage. Many never intended to kill or do any harm but because a spirit of anger dwells in them, this makes them become a murderer.

Anger is very disastrous. Many marriages have gone beyond repairs because one of the couple overreacted in anger. They were not patient and they reacted without thinking. Anger is temporary madness. Anger leads to a life of regret. Many have reacted in anger and later come to regret their action. Many have resigned from profitable jobs in anger and have lost very good opportunities. Because of uncontrolled anger, many have lost great chances in life.

When the spirit of anger takes hold of some people, you had better run and take cover. This is because whatever they lay their hands upon, they can use it on you. There was a home where the husband

and wife permitted the spirit of anger: the consequence was dire and they both lived to regret it.

One day I came home after a Sunday service, and I saw someone drove in a terribly battered car into the compound. It was a Porsche, a very special car. Someone had given this man money to go and bring this car from outside Lagos, and then he and his wife have problems and the wife descended on the new car and broke everything in it and destroyed it.

It is **anger** that makes a man rush into the house at the moment he is angry with his wife, unpack all the **certificates** that she had suffered to obtain for many years and burn them to ashes. It is the same madness that makes the wife rush into the same house, gather all the husband's clothes and set them ablaze. In this type of fiery environment, everybody is a loser.

It is anger that will make a woman throw her husband's television set from a 3-storey building. It is anger that will make a man dump his wife's phone in the toilet. It is anger that will make a woman pack out of her matrimonial home at the slightest provocation and go back to her parent's house. It is anger that makes a man lift up his hand to slap his wife. Any man that beats his wife needs **deliverance**; if you call yourself a man and you are beating your wife, you need serious deliverance!

It is anger that makes a man refuse to eat the food that his wife prepared at home: he is hungry but does not want to eat, then when he is coming home, he brings a nylon bag from the eatery, and refuses to eat the meal that he already gave his wife money to prepare! This doesn't make sense at all. Some people will even refuse to eat and sleep like that till the next day.

The other time, a man didn't want to eat the food in the house, so he went to bed in hunger. In the middle of the night, he became so hungry that he couldn't sleep. So, while everybody was sleeping, he tiptoed to the kitchen and gathered the leftover food and was about to start eating. Then his wife heard the noise in the kitchen and said, "Who is that in my kitchen?". The man opened his mouth and replied that he just came to look for his torch. He then left the kitchen and went back to bed. But still, he couldn't sleep. This happened in a house where the man is paying the rent and where he drops feeding allowance. What kind of anger is that?

Anger is like a **cancer**; it eats up its host. It burns like fire, it consumes the person bottling it up. Anger is like an **acid** that can do more harm to the vessel in which it is stored than anything on which it is poured. By the time anger was through with Moses, he had lost his chances with God. The Bible says he prayed to God and God says he should not talk to Him about the matter again.

There was a king called King Ahasuerus in the Bible. He was the King of Persia. He has a wife called Vashti. One day, the king called to his wife to come and present herself before his guests but the wife refused to come. The king did not find out if that is actually what the woman said. In anger, he said he didn't want to set his eyes on her again. But later in chapter 2, the Bible says he came to himself and regretted what he said, but it was too late (Esther 1 and 2).

Types of Anger and How to Avoid Them

Explosive anger: This is like a gas cooker or a keg of gunpowder.

Passive anger: This one is very dangerous. It is bottled up inside and it is only waiting for the day it will be provoked.

Overwhelming anger: This is the kind of anger that comes on a person because of the challenges and difficulties of life, and the person does not know how to control it.

Volatile anger: You should just run from anybody that is exhibiting this type of anger because whatever he or she is holding in his hand, he will use it on you.

Aggressive anger: This is the type that is very militant and confrontational.

Judgemental anger: This is the type that carries out a specific action against another person in vengeance. It is often for an evil purpose.

Self-inflicted anger: This is the type of anger that makes an angry person kill or harm himself or herself.

Chronic anger: This is the type of anger or emotion that is in a person for a long time, gradually destroying him or her.

Vengeful anger: This is the type of anger that resides in unforgiving people. They may be laughing with you but they are just waiting for an opportunity to avenge a past hurt.

Incidental anger: This is the anger or emotion that occurs as a result of a particular incident in a person's life.

Righteous anger: This is the anger you direct at an object of attack or offense. It is the kind of anger you direct to the devil and the spirit that is working against a person. It is often godly and positive.

Inherited anger: This is the type of emotional outburst that runs in a lineage, from parents to their children. In some families, when someone becomes angry, you must look for palm oil and put it on the head of the angry person for him to cool down.

All the spiritual marriage killers listed above are very dangerous and they portend grave danger to the homes and marital destinies of believers. It is only by prayers and watchful vigilance that children of God can overcome and destroy the insidious activities of these marriage killers.

Prayer Points

My marriage will not be a candidate of marriage wasters, in the name of Jesus.

My marriage is sealed and secured in the blood of Jesus.

Every attachment of spirit husband/wife in my marriage, fire of the God of Elijah, consume it now, in the name of Jesus.

Every certificate of demonic marriage that the enemy claims they are married to me is having, I set it on fire, in the name of Jesus.

Any power claiming I am married to him/her in the spirit, die now, in the name of Jesus.

Any power that is programming the spirit of anger into my life in order to destroy my life, be destroyed by the thunder of God, in the name of Jesus.

Every spirit that takes over me which makes me lose control of myself, I pray right now that that spirit be destroyed, in the name of Jesus.

Any bout of anger that will make me do foolish things against my marital destiny, be destroyed today, in the name of Jesus.

CHAPTER 3:

THE WAR AGAINST MARRIAGE KILLERS II

Agreement in Christian Marriage

The Bible says in the book of Amos 3:3, "Can two walk together, except they be agreed?" The Importance of unity is also emphasized in Mark 3:25 which says, "And if a house be divided against itself, that house cannot stand"

Do you want your house to stand and not be pulled down by marriage killers? Then you have to live in **unity** with your spouse. The Bible says that the house that is divided against itself will not stand. This means from inside the house, there must be no

termite that is eating up the blessing of the marriage. There must be no **scorpion** that is biting the glory of the marriage. There must be no **serpent** that is swallowing the virtue of the marriage.

Marriage, as we have been told severally, is God's first **institution** on earth. God ordained the institution for the **benefit, happiness** and **joy** of mankind. The Bible says marriage is for **honour** (Heb.13:4). Marriage is also for **glory** and **beauty**. It is for **joy** and not for sorrow. Marriage is the coming together of two persons: a husband and a wife, a man and a woman, in agreement, to be with each other till death do them part. And neither of them is complete without the other.

However, no matter how brilliant, educated, rich and endowed a man is, without a helpmate, he is not complete in the sight of God. None of the couple is complete without the other. The Bible says **two are better than one**: when they sleep together they generate heat. So, according to the wisdom of God, the coming together of the two is better than one. That is why the Bible says, **woe to that man who is alone**, because that man is at risk. When he falls, there will be nobody to help him up (Eccl.4:9-11).

In life, you cannot operate all by yourself. You will need others, but let me say this: **satan**, the archenemy of man hates marriage with perfect hatred. The devil knows the position and importance of marriage to the well-being of mankind and he will do anything to attack the home in order to destroy marriage. This is simply because every deal of God with man, including the salvation of man, comes through the home.

If there is an agenda that God has concerning this world, it is going to come through the home. If God is going to send a deliverer, if God is going to send a prophet, if God is going to intervene in the affairs of any country or any nation, it has to be through the home, and satan does not want this.

Many times, instead of Christians coming together to fight the devil, who is a common enemy, they use this energy to fight against themselves. Rather than believing and agreeing together to collectively challenge their enemies, they are busy fighting among themselves. The Bible says although we walk in the flesh, we do not war after the flesh, as the weapon of our warfare are not carnal but because of God becomes mighty and can pull down every stronghold and power that want to rise up against us (2 Cor.10:4).

Good marriages bring joy and blessings to the couple. However, they do not just come. You have to work for it. You have to decide, whether your home will be a heaven or an oven. It is a **choice** you have to make. Make up your mind, whether your house will be a heaven on earth or an oven on earth. That is a choice because, as you know, an oven is always very hot and unbearable to live in, but when your home is like heaven on earth, you will want to go there because of the good atmosphere and serenity.

When a couple decides that they will make their home a heaven on earth, and that they will resist all the enemies who want to convert their home to an oven, then they have made a good choice.

You also have to make a choice whether you will **kick or kiss** your husband or wife; whether you want to turn him or her into a **punching bag**; you have to make a choice whether you want to **embrace** your partner or **embarrass** her. Life is a choice because there are people who have chosen to be an embarrassment to the kingdom of God. It is a choice whether we make our life a **glory** or a **story**. I have seen a husband and his wife fighting on the street. I have seen a husband and wife fighting in the church. These couples have chosen that instead of embracing themselves, they will embarrass themselves. You have got to make up your mind whether your home will be a place of **rest** or a place of **arrest**. It is a choice that you must make.

Let me emphasize the fact that your husband or your wife is not your competitor. He or she is there to **help** and to **complement** you, and not an enemy to be engaged in a combat. He or she is not the enemy you need to fight.

Men should know that their wives are not **slaves** because a slave is like a property. A slave has no feeling. You can do anything you like to a slave and you will get away with it because it is your own; you bought him or her. Also, your spouse is not a **stranger** because the Bible says the stranger will fade away and will be afraid; so your home should not be a place where the other person will be afraid of. It is a stranger that should be afraid. However, your helpmate is your **friend**, your **partner** and your **better half**; he or she is not your opponent. There should be no competition or bitterness between you.

Having this in mind then, you should work in agreement with your spouse to make your marriage succeed. A marriage does not succeed by accident; it succeeds because the **committed couple** works it out. It succeeds when you invest your best into it. It succeeds when you **make it work**, but until the two persons decide they want to make it work, nothing will work.

Understand that there is no power in heaven or on earth - no marriage destroyer or killer - that can stop a husband and wife who have decided to team up and agree to make their marriage work.

Prayer Points

Any power, introducing disagreements into my marriage, be buried today, in the name of Jesus.

Any power that wants to destroy my marital vision, such power is judged today, in Jesus' name.

Holy Spirit, take absolute control of my marriage from today onward, in the name of Jesus.

I receive the power to put to flight, all the enemies of my marital breakthrough, in the name of Jesus.

I paralyse all the marriage destroyers of my father's house, in the name of Jesus.

I paralyse all the marriage killers of my mother's house, in the name of Jesus.

Any power or personality that is digging an early grave against my marriage, fall down and die, in the name of Jesus.

CHAPTER 4:

THE CHALLENGES OF MODERN MARRIAGE

Nowadays, the marriage institution is going through a lot of challenges. The rate at which marriages are falling apart in this generation is alarming. Some people get married today and the following week, there is a divorce as a result of one challenge or the other.

What are the challenges of modern marriage and what are the ways out of these challenges? These and many more will be highlighted in this chapter.

Some Challenges of Modern Marriages

Many people believe that once you get married, all your problems are gone, but this is not true. It is noteworthy that there are challenges to overcome in every marriage. We will be discussing some of these challenges and how to overcome them.

Delay in childbirth

Delay in the conception and birth of babies has wrecked and destroyed many homes. Many homes never know peace on account of delay in getting a fruit of the womb. But what is the will of God concerning fruit of the womb in marriage?

Genesis 1:28 says, 'And...God said unto them, Be fruitful... and multiply'. God has pronounced fruitfulness on your marriage, it doesn't matter what the enemies and marriage killers are doing, they will fail. Children are the heritage of the Lord; the fruit of the womb is His reward. Children are from God. If you check the Bible very well, you will see that the matter of delay in childbirth is not a new thing.

We celebrate Abraham today because he was there. Isaac was there, and also Jacob. The Bible also records the case of Elkanah and Hannah; we also read about Elizabeth and Zechariah.

For Isaac, the Bible says instead of the matter of childbirth to become a fight in the house, he took it upon himself to call upon the name of the Lord and to seek His face with fasting and praying rather than engaging in blaming and fighting with his wife. The Bible says that Isaac entreated God and God was entreated of him and the problem was solved. Most times, it is our attitude to the problem that matters and not another person's problem. The attitude of many couples is that it is the other person that is responsible: the other person is my problem; the other person is the one at fault.

Many couples need to know that the will of God is for their marriage to be fruitful, so the delay is never a denial. Check the Bible very well and you will discover that ardent believers and worshippers, like Zechariah and Elizabeth, continued serving God despite delay in the area of childbearing. Zechariah went about his business and carried on with his priestly duties in the temple as if there was no problem. At the end of the day, God remembers the aged couple and gave them a glorious child - John the Baptist - who is the forerunner of the Lord Jesus Christ.

Delay in childbirth is mostly the first challenge in a marriage, and if not properly handled, can become a big issue, especially in Africa, where a great priority is placed on children.

Financial or money problems

The irony of money is that when it is too much, there is a problem. When it is also not enough, there is a problem. That is why, in the first place, if you don't have a job and you don't have the means by which money comes in, you are not advised to get married. The reason is that God ensured that Adam had a job before He brought in a wife for him. It was not a matter of wife first. Adam already had a job he was doing before God said, "Okay, I will provide a helpmate for him". This is very important. The Bible says in 1 Timothy 5:8: *"If a man cannot provide for his family, he is worse than an unbeliever."*

This is a major problem that most men are facing nowadays.

A similar issue is one spouse earning more money than the other. Let me say this: no matter how hard two people are working, it is a fact that one will earn more than the other. There are wives who are working and will have more money than the husband; but let me say this, if you are a husband, your wife may be earning more than you, there is no crime in that. But no matter how small the money is, make sure something from your pocket enters into your wife's hand monthly for housekeeping. This carries the blessings and favour of God. Make it your habit, and God will begin to open financial doors for you.

Children's Discipline

The issue of children's discipline has caused a lot of problems in many homes. Do you know what the Bible says in Proverbs 22:6? *"Train up a child in the way he should go: and when he is old, he will not depart from it."*

We are living in a very challenging world and the forces that are against children are too much. The powers that want to destroy your home and publicly disgrace you using your children are multiplying every day. There are parents who have done what they could do; I mean by all means they tried. But their children still turned out the other way. The point there is, the responsibility is still in our hands to try more; to make sure that these children are trained in the way of the Lord.

In the Bible, Eli did not have a problem with God but where he missed it was in the area of training his children. Eli did not take decisive steps against the wayward behavior of his children who were going behind the altar to collect bribes from the church members and to sleep with women on the altar. Eli did not remove them from the job they were doing. He did not discipline them until God became angry and made the bad pronouncement on his family.

In the training of our children, we must not be found wanting. One thing we need to know is that many of these children are much smarter than we are. They can divide the home if you are not careful. Sometimes these children can play and use one parent against the other. Therefore, in the matter of training children, the couple must use a single voice: not that the man is saying this and the woman goes behind to say another thing. If you do this, you will be working at cross-purposes against each other.

Time away at work

Nowadays, couples do not have time again for romance, or to be together. This is worse when the man gets a job that transfers him away from his marriage. There are jobs that will make the man leave the house in the morning and he will not come back until late in the night when all the children are sleeping. There are jobs that place a man or a woman permanently outside the home. These jobs have destroyed many homes and they put the children at the mercy of whoever is available. This may be the househelp, the neighbor or even the television set, and these things are the causes of a lot of problems.

The social media such as the internet, mobile phones, iPad, Facebook

You need to know that no matter how good social media is, it cannot replace human beings. Many parents buy mobile devices for their children and leave them at the mercy of the internet. But as the other persons he or she is relating with are not physically available, the child using this medium will still be lonely and this poses a great challenge to him or her.

The Challenge of evil friends, families and colleagues

This influence of bad friends and family members has torn many homes apart. The son of David called Amnon was not corrupt; he didn't know how to rape girls until he listened to the counsel of his wicked friend called Jonadab who advised him to forcefully have carnal knowledge of his half-sister, Tamar (2 Samuel 13). Many homes have been destroyed, in like manner, on account of evil counsel and satanic advice from so-called friends and family members.

Lack of Godly Mentors

In the modern day, our mentors are mainly television stars in Nollywood movies. Many people have a mental fixation and base their action and lifestyle on the character of these actors, not knowing that it is not the real person they are watching.

The real one is the one you have in your house; the one you are watching on the television is not real. The Nollywood actors are just acting. A man can just walk in there and act the part on the television that encourages sex before marriage, and you might not know that this act is not of God, and it is not good and that it is something you should not emulate. The unmarried cohabiting couples you are watching on the television set are spreading an ungodly act. These are some of the challenges of this present day.

House-help Issues

Because of the busy schedule of the husband and wife, someone is often employed to come around to assist them in doing the house chores, but many of these househelps have turned out to become house problems. In many cases, it is the house-helpers who are permanently available and are attending to the husband; she is the one the husband sees every time, instead of the wife. In fact, some homes have been left for the house-help to run, to the extent that she washes everything including the man's underwear. Now, after washing the man's underwear, what else would she not wash? She will just say to herself, "If I can wash the underwear, let me do the other one too!". Many marriages therefore end up in the grave because of these house-breakers. Apart from that, some of these househelps are agents of the devil who are sent to destroy the homes. We have seen many marriages that are broken and it was later discovered that the person who is living with them is an agent of darkness.

Many times, it is the house-help that will invite the robbers to come and rob the home. Many times these monsters molest the children sexually. Many times, it is the housemaid that will take the baby away to sell to child traffickers and then the parents would be in trouble. This is a challenging time, and we need to watch out.

Some people don't really need house-helps. It is pure laziness that is worrying them. With a little re-arrangement of their schedule, they can do what most of these house-helps are paid to do. This is very important as some of these wicked house-helps have turned many families into an emergency war zone.

Cohabitation

Cohabitation is another problem of the modern man which is destroying the marriage institution. This evil practice is very prevalent now. Young men and women do not follow the traditional marriage rites or church marriage again. Nothing is done to signify their commitment or respect for the marriage institution; they just get an apartment and start to sleep together under the same roof. If you ask what they are doing, they will reply that they are trying to see whether they are compatible with each other.

Solutions To Marital Challenges

The first way to resolve your marital challenge is to know and practice all God's rules and commandments concerning marriage. The second way is to remember your marriage vows. Remember the day you stood before God and the church congregation and the man of God read those terrible words (marriage vows) to you and instead of you to say no, you opened your mouth and said yes. The priest or pastor stood before you and said "Man, will you take this woman as your lawfully wedded wife?". You said, "Yes, I will". Then you went ahead to say, "I will protect and love her, for better for worse; for richer, for poorer; in sickness and in good health…". This means you heard what the man of God said, you understood the language he spoke to you and you agreed to abide by the vow. So, you are already inside, there's no coming out.

If you are married, turn back to God and ask Him to give you the divine wisdom to manage your marital affairs. He is the Author and Founder of the marriage establishment, and He will help you. Remember the vows you made on your wedding day. No matter what challenges that come your way, stay true and faithful to these vows. This is very important because the words of this vow will either stand for or against you on the dreadful Day of Judgment.

May you be divinely guided to face your marital challenges and make good decisions to overcome them, in Jesus' name.

Prayer Points

Any power that wants my marriage to scatter, I command you to scatter, in the name of Jesus.

Heavens over my finances, open today, in the name of Jesus.

Heavens of marital favor, open over me today, in the name of Jesus.

I command any satanic force troubling my marriage to fall down and die, in the name of Jesus.

My Father, my Father endue me with divine wisdom to make good decisions that will take my marriage forward, in Jesus' name.

Divine power to overcome all marital challenges, fall upon me now, in the name of Jesus.

I destroy the activities of marriage destroyers over my life, in the name of Jesus.

CHAPTER 5:

CHARACTERISTICS OF GODLY MARRIAGES

If God says something is not good, there are no experts, no wisdom, no knowledge, and no counsel that can make it good. God said it is not good that a man should be alone (Gen. 2:18). He said He will make a suitable helper for him, who will be exactly like himself and who will help him so that both can live a fulfilled life.

After establishing the marriage institution, God gave specific instructions on how a man and woman are to live in order to enjoy the marriage and please Him. As a result of this, there are certain characteristics that can be used to identify godly marriages.

Characteristics of Godly Marriages

It is ordained by God.

The first thing you need to know is that marriage is not man's idea, but a respectable and dignified institution ordained by God.

It is deep and mysterious.

Marriage is a mystery. The coming together of a man and a woman to produce godly seeds that will fit into the will and purpose of God on earth is a deep mystery which the devil and his cohort cannot comprehend (Gen. 3:15; Rev. 12:17).

It is a cure for loneliness.

God instituted marriage as a solution to cure loneliness, depression, and sorrow. He brought Eve to Adam as a helpmate in the Garden of Eden to help him fulfill his destiny.

It provides support and care.

It is in marriage that you find support and care to fulfill life and destiny. The Bible says woe to that man that is alone because when he falls, there will be nobody to help him up. The Bible says two are better than one because they will always have the rewards of their labor; it says when two people are together, they generate heat, they are warm, they share ideas, they get strength from each other.

It is a union of the hearts.

According to the Bible, God made Adam sleep and He took one of the bones of his ribs, and from the ribs, He made Eve. Note where the Lord took the bone from: He didn't take the bone from the head, He didn't take the bone from the legs, He didn't take the bone from the spinal cord, but He took it from the ribs, close to the heart. So, marriage is a matter of the heart. That is why they call the partners soul mates. Marriage is the matter of the heart and it involves friendship, intimacy, accord, affection, mutuality, friendship, agreement, unity, etc. The person you marry is supposed to occupy your heart. You are supposed to place the person you marry uppermost in your heart too. So, it is a heart affair, it is not a leg affair, a head affair, or an arm affair. Until your marriage affects your heart, the most intimate part of you, you cannot make a success of it. Remember, it is not the bone from the buttock, it is not the bone from the legs, it is the bone from the heart that God used to fashion your spouse: that is why you call her 'sweetheart'.

Marriage is based on God's love and not on material things.

Any marriage that is established on any other thing apart from God's love will not stand, any marriage that is established on material things will not stand the test of time, it will collapse and fall. Marriage must be based on love. That is, godly love. It is only love that can keep a marriage for a long time. It is only love that can sustain a marriage; it is only love that can blend a marriage together. Marriage can only be sustained by love, and the Bible says love is always patient, love is kind, love is not selfish, and there is love in sharing. When the challenges of life come against a marriage, the only thing that will keep the marriage strong and standing is love. When love is not there, and the marriage is based on physical or material things, the marriage will not stand. Certainly, the flood and trials will come, but when the marriage is rooted in the love of God, it will stand the test of time.

Marriage is the union of two people who forgive easily

Neither of the parties is perfect because nobody is an angel. It is not allowed in this side of eternity that angels should marry, only men and women marry, so that person you marry is not an angel. She must certainly have her fault, he must certainly have his faults; he will certainly have his weaknesses, and you will certainly have your weaknesses, so our ability to recognize and to resolve all these things within the confines of marriage is very important. The Bible says offenses will come (Luke 17:1); you may call the man a gentleman but it is just a matter of time, offenses will come.

8. The devil hates the marriage of Christians

The enemy is not happy at all about the marriage of Christians and will do everything to work against it. A Christian brother was inside a plane some years back and he noticed that the man that was beside him kept declining all the different foods they bring for him; he refused to eat any. This Christian brother was concerned and after sometime, he asked the man if he was observing a Christian fast. The man replied that he was not a Christian. He said he belonged to a particular occult group and they are fasting to make sure that Christian marriages and homes are pulled down. Sometimes in life, there are forces we cannot see. That is why man's capacity alone cannot sustain marriage. What you have learnt in school cannot sustain your marriage. Your romantic text messages cannot sustain your marriage. What you need is the power of God. To get this, you need to pray. That is why prayer is very important in marriage. You need the grace and protective arm of God to keep your family together and it has always been said that a family that prays together stays together. So, you need prayer to ward off all the evil arrows that the enemies are firing into your marriage. The couple must pray for each other because the Bible says the weapons of our warfare are not carnal but are mighty through Christ to the pulling down of strongholds. It is through prayer that Christian couples can deal with those forces that are working against their marriages.

Marriage is a union between a mature adult male(man) and female(woman)

The sad reality of homosexuality ravaging the world today is as a result of the devil's ceaseless attack on the institution of marriage. From the scripture, we read that marriage is between a man (Adam) and a woman (Eve); it is not between John and James, and it is not between Adam and Steve. In Mark 6:10, the Bible says, "...*from the beginning of creation God made them male and female.*" It says in verse 7: "*For this cause shall a man (male) leave his father and mother, and cleave to his wife (female)."* The devil wants to destroy this world by usurping the divine institution of marriage. How do you feel when you see two men who claim they are married and are kissing each other? It is such an ugly sight! I am sure you feel like you want to vomit? It doesn't make sense when you see a man calling another man his wife. I always feel like I should see a bow and arrow and shoot them in the eyes, because it is such an ugly sight. May God deliver us from this abomination, in Jesus' name.

The situation we are facing now is not normal at all. If you ask these people, *"Your father that gave birth to you, if he had married a man, would he have given birth to you?"*, they will refuse to answer you. Homosexuality is therefore an attack against the word of God who says, *"Be fruitful, and multiply, and replenish the earth."* Now, the same people want to adopt children, children born by the normal husband and wife.

If you are not interested in obeying God, why are you looking for the fruit of the womb which only the Lord can give? May the Lord deliver this generation, in the name of Jesus.

It is a terrible sight to see a woman and a woman playing husband and wife. It is a demonic thing. How on earth can a man say he doesn't have feelings for the opposite sex but for a man like himself? May you not experience this in the life of your children. May this demonic spirit not enter into any of your family members.

There is no room for divorce in a Christian marriage:

In a Christian marriage, there is no room for divorce. The Bible says, "...*till death do you part*". God also says that, "*he hateth putting away*" (Mal. 2:16). One day, some people asked Jesus what Moses said about giving a letter of divorcement to a woman and sending her away. Jesus replied that the person who created the marriage institution (God), from the beginning did not make provision for divorce and that it was Moses who introduced this, and that it is not in the original program of God. God hates putting away. He hates divorce with perfect hatred. Jesus told his disciples in Mark 10:11-12: *"Whosoever shall put away his wife and marry another, committeth adultery against her. And if a woman shall put away her husband, and be married to another, she committeth adultery."*

The reason why marriage is very important to God is that every program of His falls within the context of marriage. When man fell, God said to the woman that her seed would eventually fill the earth, so salvation is rooted inside the family. Deliverance of mankind is inside the family, and when Jesus Christ was on earth, He performed His first miracle at a marriage ceremony: in Cana of Galilee, where He was invited along with His disciples, brothers, and mother. This tells us how important the matter of marriage is to God.

There is a country in the world today, if you want to get a divorce there, it is as easy as going to an ATM and pressing a button that your marriage is not working, you have changed your mind about it and you are terminating it. Then you pay the normal fee and that will be the end of the marriage. This shows how easy it is to get a divorce in the world now, especially in a country like Spain. But divorce is not an option in a Christian marriage. God hates divorce, so Christian couples must do everything they can to resolve their differences and destroy the devil's plan in their lives.

Marriage requires diligence and great effort to succeed

Every believer must work hard to make sure that his or her marriage succeeds. For a marriage to succeed requires great effort; a great marriage requires hard work and diligence, and the couple has to keep on learning. At no point can they finish learning because marriage is a lifelong school. The man and woman should realize that they are yet to learn everything about each other and so enroll in the school of continuous learning.

A lady must be naïve to think that the way the man behaved towards her during courtship is the way he is going to behave when she marries him. It must be realized that the courtship period is a phase, while the marriage is another phase, and the couple must adapt accordingly.

All believers must seek the mind of God for His will about their marital destiny. This may require prolonged praying and fasting. But this is a great investment that will be rewarded by the Founder of the marriage institution, who alone knows how to give good and perfect gifts to His children (James 1:17).

Prayer Points

O Lord my Father, give me the grace to know and to do Your will for my life, in the name of Jesus.

I receive the power to operate with sharp spiritual eyes that cannot be deceived, in the name of Jesus.

O God of Elijah, give me the power to know deep and secret things concerning my marital destiny, in the name of Jesus.

O God my Father, show me the blueprint for my marriage, in the name of Jesus.

Lord, make Your way plain unto me concerning my marriage, in the name of Jesus.

Father Lord, reveal to me secrets that will move my marital destiny forward, in the name of Jesus.

My marital destiny, come out of the covens of darkness into the mountaintop of fulfillment, in the name of Jesus.

LADEJOLA ABIODUN

CHAPTER 6:

TEN COMMANDMENTS OF GODLY MARRIAGE

There are ten divine Commandments concerning marriage. Take note of these commandments and let them guide you in your daily matrimonial decisions. If you observe these Ten Commandments, they will make your marriage stronger and fruitful. By taking cognizance of these Commandments, you will be able to destroy the activities of marriage destroyers that are waging war against your marital progress.

1. Thou shall forgive thy spouse as many times as he or she offends you.

When the disciples of Jesus asked him how often a man should forgive another, He replied that it is 70 x 7 times. It is impossible for someone to offend you 70 x 7 times in a day or even in a year. The truth that Jesus is expressing here is that there must be a lot of forgiveness between a married couple, that is, before a person offends you, you have already forgiven him or her; before he or she confesses his or her sins, you have already expressed your desire to forgive her. This is what Christ teaches (Matt. 18:22). May God give us the power to put this into practice.

2. Honour thy father-in-law and your mother-in-law but thou shall endeavour to cut their string or rope of control.

You are duty-bound to honour your father-in-law and your mother-in-law, but make sure that you cut yourself loose from their string or rope of control that they want to use to control your home. This is a practicable thing and should not be difficult for you to do. Do not allow anybody to control your home. You must be man enough to ward off any evil influence over your marriage. It is a great embarrassment if you are not bold enough to manage your marital problems and you are involving external forces or third parties to intervene in your affairs. Some mother-in-laws are so dominant that when they come to visit their sons, they sack the wife and take over the marriage bed, and sleep beside their own sons and chase the wife away. If this is happening to you, you are not yet a man and marriage is not meant for boys like you. You should love your parents but you should not permit their control over your home; draw a line and learn to say, "Sorry, this is my home; this is my wife; this is my husband…" May the lord help us, in Jesus' name.

3. Thou shall have no other person beside your spouse.

This means no other person is permitted to be closer to more than your spouse. It is not good for you as a married man, to be closer to your sister or mother than your wife, or to fill a form and put your sister or mother as your next of kin. If you do this, you are not obeying the commandment of God.

Adultery and infidelity are totally forbidden in a Christian marriage, because they have terrible consequences. Be content with what you have that God has given you. There is nothing you are looking for that your husband or wife does not have. The Bible says the two of them (the man and his wife) shall become one flesh. No other woman is allowed to be closer to you than your wife, no other man is allowed to be closer to you than your husband, not your mother or your father or even the children. Some women love and place more priority on their children over their husbands. This is wrong. You should know that these children will grow up and leave you one day, but you and your spouse will live together for life. Therefore, the spousal love between the wife and the husband should be above all others.

4. Thou shall not speak evil of thy spouse, but shall love, honour and defend him or her at all times.

This means you should not speak evil, negative or unpalatable words against your spouse anywhere or at any time. The only words you are allowed to speak publicly about him or her at all times are words of commendation, praises and encouragement. You should be proud to introduce your spouse to others at any function.

5. Thou shall not carry into today the trouble of yesterday.

The scripture says you must not allow the sun to go down on your wrath (Eph. 4:26). This means you must always settle and resolve whatever problem or challenge you have with your spouse before the day runs out.

6. Thou shall not argue but discuss.

Instead of resorting to arguments, temper tantrums, shouting matches and the use of abusive words (such as 'I regret the day I met you', 'you are the worst thing that ever happened to me', etc.), the couple should learn good communication skills. They should discuss and analyze issues before the matter get out of hand.

7. Thou shall live within your financial means.

Every man has a financial level that he occupies, so, believe God to take you from the level you are now to a better and a higher level. Do not compare yourself, your husband or your wife with another person. Whatever God endows you with now, live within that means, and don't be under pressure to do something untoward. Don't put your spouse under pressure to buy this or buy that; live within your means now, and have faith in God that the future will be great. What you cannot afford today will be affordable tomorrow, therefore cut your cloth according to your size.

8. Thou shall make your marriage as romantic as possible.

You must not allow your marriage to remain dull. You must be creative and continue to come up with romantic ways to revitalize the relationship. You need to add some creative juice and pep every now and then into the marriage and do everything you can to make your marriage lively and interesting. For instance, instead of eating at home on a weekend, you can decide to go for a picnic at a nearby park where the two of you will be together.

9. Thou shall read the word of God and pray together daily.

The daily devotion in Bible reading, prayer and meditation of scripture keeps a marriage spiritually strong and godly. Prayer is necessary as it fertilizes marriages, it wards off demonic attack of unseen forces and opens the window of blessing of God for the couple. In Genesis 19:19, the Bible says concerning Abraham, that he will always command his family to follow the way of the Lord. God called Abraham his friend because he would sit with his family and instruct them in the way of God. In your home, the word of God must take a prominent place. The word of God should be supreme. Every morning, each

Christian home should share the word of God and pray. By doing this, God will take the marriage to greater and greater heights.

10. Thou shall not use sex as a weapon of punishment against your spouse.

The Bible says to married couples: "defraud ye not one another, except it be with consent for a time, that ye may give yourselves to fasting and prayer; and come together again, so that Satan tempt you not for your incontinency" (1 Cor. 7:5). The Bible added that immediately after the prayer, you should quickly come together again so that the devil will not tempt you. Sex should not be used as an instrument of exchange, by which the lady will say, 'If you want it, sign this cheque'. One pastor once revealed that one day before they had sex, his wife threatened and forced him to sign a cheque and he signed it, but after the sex, he also retaliated by placing a call to his bank manager that the cheque should not be honoured. This type of cat-and-dog lifestyle is unbecoming of good Christian couples.

Prayer Points

1. I fire back every arrow of sudden death targeted against my marriage, in the name of Jesus.

2. Owners of evil marital load, appear and carry your load, in the name of Jesus.

3. Every curse of 'thou shall not excel' over my marriage, break, in the name of Jesus.

4. Stronghold of delay working against my marriage, I pull you down, in the name of Jesus.

5. Every witchcraft covenant working against my marriage, break, in the name of Jesus.

6. Father, make my home an example of a good Christian home, in the name of Jesus.

7. Any power waging war against my marriage, die, in the name of Jesus.

8. Witchcraft attacks against my marriage, as I clap my hands now, receive the thunder of God, in the name of Jesus.

9. Any power, claiming to be my wife/husband, I am not your wife/husband, release me and die, in the name of Jesus.

10. Weapon of manipulation employed against my marriage, catch fire, in the name of Jesus.

11. My marriage, I prophesy unto you, you shall not fail, in the name of Jesus.

12. Any mirror of darkness that is being used to remotely control my home, break to pieces, in the name of Jesus.

13. Any power chewing kolanut and chanting incantation to scatter my family, fall down and die, in the name of Jesus.

14. Because I am here today, and because the spirit of God is here, every local bondage, acquired bondage, transferred bondage, and projected

bondage into my marriage is broken, in the name of Jesus.

15. Every covenant of delay, programmed into my marriage by ancestral marine spirit: because the spirit of God is here, I am freed from them all, in the name of Jesus.

16. The chain with which the enemy has locked me and my family, I command the chain to break now, in the name of Jesus.

17. Any power assigned to kill good things in my life and in my marriage, be destroyed by fire, in the name of Jesus.

18. Begin to thank God for answers to all the prayers.

LADEJOLA ABIODUN

CONCLUSION

In Malachi 2:14-15, the Bible says, "Yet ye say, Wherefore? Because the Lord had been witness between thee and the wife of thy youth, against whom thou hast dealt treacherously: yet is she thy companion, and the wife of thy covenant. And did not he make one? Yet had he the residue of the spirit. And wherefore one? That he might seek a godly seed. Therefore take heed to your spirit, and let none deal treacherously with the wife of his youth."

From this passage, God is saying, "I am a witness; I am an independent observer, I am around and I am taking records. Whatever you are doing in this marriage, my eyes are on you, don't think that nobody is taking record of what you are doing. He says, "I am taking record, so behave well and be careful the way you handle the wife of your youth, the way you handle the husband of your youth."

Don't imagine that what you do here on earth will not be accounted for. Note that there is a day that we shall all be accountable for all our deeds. Marriage is ordained by God. It is designed for honor and not for shame. It is designed for pleasure and not for pressure. Marriage is for glory and not for groaning. Marriage is a cure for loneliness. The Bible says, *"He setteth the solitary in families..."* (Psalm 68:6).

Marriage is given to make man better and not to make him bitter. He says, *"It is not good that a man should be alone"* (Gen. 2:18). Can you imagine what it will look like if you are all alone? The Bible also says, *"Two are better than one because they will have reward for their labour, and that if one is weak, the other will strengthen him..."*

God gives marriage to man in order to bless man. It is a blessing from the Almighty God. He says, *"Whoso findeth a wife findeth a good thing, and obtaineth favour of the Lord."* So, marriage is wedlock and not a padlock. Neither the man nor the woman is complete without the other. The two are better than one.

The word of God says, for this purpose a man will leave his father and his mother and cleave unto his wife and the two shall become one. Marriage involves leaving and cleaving, unfortunately many marriages are not free today because of external control and powerful dominance of the in-laws and relatives who will not let go.

The greatest force on this earth is a prayer of agreement between a husband and his wife. The Bible says if two shall agree and ask for anything, God will do it (Amos 3:3; Mark 16:17). It further says that one will chase a thousand and two will chase ten thousand. The devil hates this force being put to use because he knows that he will be defeated. So he would do everything to make sure that this force does not come to effect.

There is an evil statistic that says 50 percent of modern marriages end in divorce between the first and fifth year. 20 percent of marriages are already divorced, and between 40 to 50 percent do not live to witness the 15th anniversary.

Your marriage shall not be added to this evil statistic, in the name of Jesus.

WHAT YOU NEED TO DO TO ENJOY A GODLY MARRIAGE

Understand who your partner is.

This is done over a long time. In fact, getting to know your partner is a lifetime thing. You keep on discovering new things about him or her, and knowing him/her better and better every day of your lives.

Destroy the spirit of anger in your life.

It is softness, understanding, and patience that make a marriage work. Learning to cultivate the virtue of patience is very important. That is what you bring to a marriage. If you have an anger issue, see a man of God or a Christian counselor to help you resolve it. The Bible says in Ephesians 4:31, *"Let all bitterness, and wrath, and anger, and clamour, and evil speaking, be put away from you, with all malice. And be ye kind one to another, tenderhearted, forgiving one another, even as God for Christ's sake hath forgiven you."*

Keep your voice low when you are having a discussion with your spouse.

Good and reasonable communication is important in any relationship, and you don't need to shout to achieve this. The Bible says in the book of Proverbs that a gentle answer turns away wrath (Prov. 15:1). Learn to respond gently and be patient with your wife, and you will gain her trust, confidence, and intimacy.

Be tolerant.

There are certain things you cannot change in the life of your partner. Ask God for the grace to live with those things you cannot change. This is very important.

Make sure you forgive quickly and easily.

Make up your mind that your marriage will not be added to the bad statistical record of failed marriages in the world today. Forgive and erase all offenses and perceived slights. Do not keep any record of these. By doing so, you will be obeying the injunction of Christ and will not give the devil and marriage killers any foothold in your home.

Make prayer your steering wheel and not your spare tire.

The forces (marriage killers) that are against your marital destiny are much. This means that you as a couple need to stay together and pray together. You need to pray against such things as disunity, the activities of strange men and women, and the evil plan of the enemy concerning your marriage. This is very important.

Let the Holy Spirit lead and guide you at all times.

The Bible says, *"For as many as are led by the Spirit of God, they are the sons of God."* (Rom. 8:14). As you pray and fellowship together, allow the Holy Spirit to lead you. Do not forget that He is the Head of every marriage; the success of your marriage depends on Him, so do not hesitate to call on Him in times of need.

LADEJOLA ABIODUN

BONUS SECTION: PROPHETIC DECLARATIONS & DECREES

DELIVERANCE FROM FOUNDATIONAL BONDAGES AND YOKES

I dethrone every queen and king of darkness ruling in my life, in Jesus' name

Organs of my body, shall not be devoured by eaters of flesh and drinkers of blood, in Jesus' name

I challenge my internal organs of my body with burning hot colds of fire, in the name of Jesus

Masquerade powers sitting on my breakthroughs, I push you off, in Jesus' name

Anything representing me in the dark world, catch fire, in Jesus' name

Problems expanders, my life will not carry problems, in Jesus' name

Strange spirits living with me in my house, the fire of destroys you now, in Jesus' name

Witchcraft pot cooking my flesh, catch fire, in Jesus' name

Serpent of poverty, I cut of your head, in Jesus' name

Spirit of failure at the edge of success, expire, in Jesus' name

Powers that want me to suffer what my parents suffer, I destroy you, in Jesus' name

Bitter water assigned to embarrass me with poverty, dry up, in Jesus' name

Serpents that swallow wealth, my life is not your candidate, in Jesus' name

Closed doors before me, hear the word of the Lord open now, in Jesus' name

Eaters and flesh, my body is not your candidate, I crush you, in Jesus' name

Any form of spiritual soul tie, break and release me, in Jesus' name

The habitation of familiar spirit in my Foundation becomes desolate, in Jesus' name

Poison of darkness that render destiny useless, come out of my body and die, in Jesus' name

The throne room of witchcraft in my family, become desolate, in Jesus' name

The activities of witchcraft in my family be terminated, in Jesus' name

Evil plantations of witchcraft in my body, come out and die, in Jesus' name

The blood of ritual and sacrifice that speaking against by moving forward, be silenced, in Jesus' name

Owner of evil loads, carry your loads now, in Jesus' name

The negative of parental idol worshiping the life and destiny, be destroyed, in Jesus' name

Every inherited mark of failure, be cut off from me, in Jesus' name

Dirty and filthy hands of witchcraft troubling my life wither, in Jesus' name

Every dark presence magnetizing problems into my life, be destroyed, in Jesus' name

Every organized warfare to strip me naked physically and spiritually, die, in Jesus' name

Whoever used my pictures to program poverty into my life shall fail, in Jesus' name

I pull down every stronghold of demonic powers in my Foundation, in Jesus' name

The witchcraft net working against me, scatter, in Jesus' name

The powers of diviners and charmers, be rendered powerless over me, in Jesus' name

Thou power of emptier, break upon my life, in Jesus' name

Witchcraft umbrella blocking favor from flowing to me, catch fire, in Jesus' name

No matter how the enemies try to wage war, their efforts shall end in failures, in Jesus' name

Negative words that have been spoken, that is affecting my life, dry up, in Jesus' name

Every dance in the palace targeted to cut off my head, scatter, in Jesus' name

My head jump out of the prison of limitation by the power in the blood of Jesus name

Evil marks making the enemy to mock me, be wiped, in Jesus' name

The sun shall not smite me by the neither the moon by night, in Jesus' name

By the wonderworking power of Jesus, every stubborn problem in my life, expire, in Jesus' name

Arrows of delay celebration, go back to where you are coming from, in Jesus' name

Witchcraft padlocks militating against me break to pieces, in Jesus' name

The eagle of my glory, you cannot remain where you are, arise and shine, in Jesus' name

Powers feeding me with the bread of sorrow and water of affliction, die, in Jesus' name

Frustration and disappointment shall not be my portion, in Jesus' name

Powers supply my enemies with bullets to fire at me, thunder of God, strike them, in Jesus' name

Altars of witchcraft, monitoring my progress, catch fire, in Jesus' name

Foundational problems on assignment to disgrace me, wither, in Jesus' name

Where ever I have been tied down, Holy Ghost fire, set me, free, in Jesus' name

BREAKING THE HOLD OF FAMILY IDOL AND ANCESTRAL STRONGMAN

Powers that are claiming that I have been handed to him, you are a liar, die, in Jesus' name

I cancel every conscious and unconscious marriage agreement with any dark power, in the name of Jesus

Power using the hours of the night to pollute my life and marriage die

Every yoke that says I shall not be more than this break, in Jesus' name

Witchcraft embargo on my glorious destiny, break, in Jesus' name

Every curse that is programmed to begin to affect me negatively at a particular time of life break, in Jesus' name

Every curse that says money shall not met money in my hands break, in Jesus' name

Every curse that says I will serve others, nobody will serve me, wither, in Jesus' name

The season of my rain of abundance begin to manifest now, in Jesus' name

O God, by your possibility power, make impossible possible in my life, in Jesus' name

I ruin the association of familiar spirits gather to do me harm, in Jesus' name

Destructive arrow of darkness fired against me, backfire, in Jesus' name

Night arrow assigned to destroy my blessings during the day, backfire, in Jesus' name

Witchcraft forceful initiation be render to nothing, in Jesus' name

My bondages, I command you to enter into your bondage, in Jesus' name

The image of demons programmed to torment me in the dream, be destroyed, in Jesus' name

Projection of domestic witchcraft fashioned against any organ of my body, in Jesus' name

Every pot of sacrifices carried to do me harm, catch fire, in Jesus' name

The Lord God Almighty shall make a way for me where there is no way, in Jesus' name

Witchcraft animals swallowing my wealth die, in Jesus' name

Let the arrows of witchcraft organized for my sake backfire, in Jesus' name

I shall not be forgotten, where I am supposed to be remembered, in Jesus' name

The serpent of the magician swallowing my breakthroughs, I kill you with the sword of fire, in Jesus' name

Witchcraft burial conducted against me in any coven, expire, in Jesus' name

Witchcraft cage holding anything that belongs to me, release it now, in Jesus' name

Evil veil covering my eyes from seeing what I am supposed to see catch fire, in Jesus' name

Every pot of enchantment against me, break to pieces, in Jesus' name

My blessing, come out of the cage of witchcraft, in Jesus' name

Satanic priest operating any dark altar against me, fall down and die, in Jesus' name

Every power of witchcraft cooking my flesh, break to pieces, in Jesus' name

Agenda of envious witchcraft targeted against me, die, in Jesus' name

The crying blood against my success and progress be silenced, in Jesus' name

Every household witchcraft employing fetish power against me, wither, in Jesus' name

My spirit, soul and body shall not be bewitched, in Jesus' name

BREAKING EVIL SOUL TIE

I break the yoke of ancestral soul tie holding me down, in Jesus' name

The curse of perpetual slavery working against me, break, in Jesus' name

Covenant of blood and sacrifice keeping problem in place in my life, be dissolved, in Jesus' name

Powers that have vowed that they would rather die, than seen prosper, die, in Jesus' name

Every soul tie with any man living or dead, break, in Jesus' name

The covenant of the blood of Jesus, deliver me evil family pattern, in Jesus' name

Powers that make good things to jump over me, come out of me, in Jesus' name

Witchcraft embargo of thou shall not excel placed on my life, break, in Jesus' name

Every blood tie with familiar or ancestral spirit, break, in Jesus' name

Every ancient prison house, let me go, in Jesus' name

Evil word spoken by the wicked that troubling my life, wither, in Jesus' name

Venom of serpent and scorpion, come out of me, in Jesus' name

Seasonal battle assigned to stop my breakthroughs, die, in Jesus' name

Witchcraft marks suppressing my personal testimony, clear away, in Jesus' name

O God make haste and bring me out satanic detention, in Jesus' name

Power enforcing satanic wishes on my life, die, in Jesus' name

The voice of impossibility shouting loudly against my star, wither, in Jesus' name

Serpent that wastes effort and labor, die, in Jesus' name

Thunder fire of God break satanic cage build around my life, in Jesus' name

Crippling power in my foundation, die, in Jesus' name

Evil covering assigned against my head, I set you ablaze, in Jesus' name

Evil arrow that paralyzed glorious destiny, go back to your sender, in Jesus' name

Padlock of darkness tying my glory die, break to pieces, in Jesus' name

Evil wind directed at me, backfire, in Jesus' name

Spell and hexes of frustration, break and release me, in Jesus' name

Evil command issued against me, my life and destiny reject you, in Jesus' name

Satanic burial done against my marriage, wither, in Jesus' name

Evil prayers made against on any altar, be canceled, in Jesus' name

Dark broom sweeping away good things from me, catch fire, in Jesus' name

I break and release from every serpent and scorpion of death, in Jesus' name

DESTROY SATANIC REMOTE CONTROLLING POWER WORKING AGAINST YOUR LIFE

The foundational strongman assigned to cripple my elevation, fall down and die, in Jesus' name

O God arise let the wicked be swallowed by the evil they have imagined against me, in Jesus' name

Every door of progress shut against me, open, in Jesus' name

Every resistance to my divine acceleration and promotion, be dashed to pieces, in Jesus' name

Thou power of emptier and waster assigned against me, be destroyed, in Jesus' name

Internal and external devices of domestic witchcraft blocking the rising of my star, burn to ashes, in Jesus' name

Serpent and scorpion of failure at the edge of success, die, in Jesus' name

No wickedness shall prevail against me, in Jesus' name

My star and glory rejects bewitchment, in Jesus' name

1Hamman diverting my breakthrough, wither, in Jesus' name

Witchcraft padlock that holds destiny down in the place of frustration, die, in Jesus' name

Association of wicked elders on assignment against my life, scatter, in Jesus' name

Evil speaking against my success, wither, in Jesus' name

O God by your power, bring me out of every valley of working without results, die, in Jesus' name

Invisible chains of environmental witchcraft in my hands, break, in Jesus' name

Satanic legislation working against me, be nullified, in Jesus' name

The concluded work of darkness against my prosperity, scatter, in Jesus' name

The key of my promotion in the hands of spiritual robbers, be released to me now, in Jesus' name

Ancestral witchcraft embargo, break, in Jesus' name

Wind of positive change blow in my favor, in Jesus' name

The wickedness of the wicked, expire today, in Jesus' name

Every satanic set up to frustrate me, be dismantled, in Jesus' name

Thou spirit of almost there but never there, assigned against me, die, in Jesus' name

In Jesus' name, I shall not die, before the manifestation of my glory, in Jesus' name

O ye gate of hell, fashioned against my progress, scatter, in Jesus' name

The rod of the wicked shall not rest upon the lot of my life, in Jesus' name

Enchantment from the sun, moon and star, fail woefully, in Jesus' name

Witchcraft handwriting, be wiped from my destiny, by the power in the blood of Jesus

Owners of the load of suffering I summon you to come and carry your loads, in Jesus' name

My original glory, where you are buried, come out and locate, in Jesus' name

DESTROY SATANIC COVENANT THAT HINDERS PROGRESS

I break covenant of limitation, in Jesus' name

What is meant to kill me, shall die in my place, in Jesus' name

No organ of my body shall be donated to dark kingdom, in Jesus' name

Powers that want to come down, I shall not come down, die, in Jesus' name

Evil gathering of the wicked against my future, scatter, in Jesus' name

The dominion of my glorious destiny shall not be crippled, in Jesus' name

The strongman that does not want my glory to rise and shine, be destroyed, in Jesus' name

I receive anointing to break forth and breakthrough, in Jesus' name

The wall Jericho standing between me and my breakthrough, fall, in Jesus' name

Failure and defeat shall not be my portion, in Jesus' name

Witchcraft burial, conducted to bury good things of my life, die, in Jesus' name

Witchcraft cage fashioned against me, break, in Jesus' name

Witchcraft warehouse, release my wealth you are holding, in Jesus' name

Witchcraft garment of demotion, I set you ablaze, in Jesus' name

Evil line the enemy says I cannot cross, I cross over by fire, in Jesus' name

Owner of the load of infirmity, carry your load, in Jesus' name

Every close chapter of my divine manifestation and intervention, open, in Jesus' Jesus name

Thou power of collective captivity, break, in Jesus' name

Holy Ghost, consume the evil seed growing in my life, in Jesus' name

Every problem that has a name in my life, wither, in Jesus' name

Blood of Jesus, dissolve satanic arrow by burning power, in Jesus' name

By the power that raised Lazarus from the death, let my stubborn problem receive solution now, in Jesus' name

I shake off sickness and disease from my body, in Jesus' name

I shake evil arrow from my destiny, in Jesus' name

I curse the root of slavery to die, in my life, in Jesus' name

Bondage expander and yoke promoter, die, in Jesus' name

Poison that leads to sudden death, come out of me, in Jesus' name

EJECTING OF POISON OF DARKNESS FROM YOUR BODY

Poison of sudden death, come out of my body, in Jesus' name

Dark plantation, come out of me, in Jesus' name

My life and destiny receive empowerment to succeed, in Jesus' name

Witchcraft poison as a result of eating polluted food, come out of me, in Jesus' name

Satanic programmed object, come out of my body, in Jesus' name

Dark table of domestic witchcraft, catch fire, in Jesus' name

Dark room caging my wealth, release my wealth, in Jesus' name

I declare war against poverty, sickness and failure, in Jesus' name

Every sickness that has a name in my life, die, in Jesus' name

Every witchcraft basket flying for me sake, catch fire, in Jesus' name

Evil arrow, programmed to any dark hour of the night against me, backfire, in Jesus' name

My life and destiny shall not be covered by darkness, in Jesus' name

My spirit, soul and body reject evil plantation, in Jesus' name

Holy Ghost, make my life conducive for your presence, in Jesus' name

Demon shall not use my body as their evil habitation, in Jesus' name

Death and destruction shall not feed on my body, in Jesus' name

Every blood speaking against my blood line, shut up and die, in Jesus' name

Every unconscious witchcraft altar, ministering against me, catch fire, in Jesus' name

Arrow of affliction fired against me, loose your hold, in Jesus' name

Where is the Lord God of Elijah, I tear down the altar of magician hired against me, in Jesus' name

Satanic dedication that speaks against my glory, be silenced, in Jesus' name

Every good thing houses I have lived in the past have stolen from me, I take it back, in Jesus' name

I vomit every dark food, I have eaten from the table of the enemy, in Jesus' name

Let every stubborn pursuer of my life turn back from me, in Jesus' name

My life, you shall not cooperate with evil designer, in Jesus' name

Chain of oppression, limiting me, break, in Jesus' name

Holy Ghost package me for Miracles, signs and wonders, in Jesus' name

O Lord, according the greatness of your power, manifest yourself in my life, in Jesus' name

My body shall not be habitation of devils, in Jesus' name

Any dark object representing me in the dark kingdom, catch fire, in Jesus' name

DELIVERANCE FROM THE SHADOW OF DEATH

Spirit of death and hell, loose your hold upon my life, in Jesus' name

Any strongman sitting on what belongs to me I push you out by fire, in Jesus' name

Every mark of slavery placed upon my life, break, in Jesus' name

Anointing of double recovery, fall upon my life, die, in Jesus' name

O God arise and single me out for your Miracles, in Jesus' name

O God arise and make haste to bless me, in Jesus' name

The enemy shall not succeed to remove me from my place of blessing, in Jesus' name

My destiny helpers where are you appear, in Jesus' name

O God rend the heaven for my sake and bless me, in Jesus' name

The spell of wrong association, break and release me, in Jesus' name

Powers that have stolen from me, give me back what you have stolen from me, in Jesus' name

Every organized warfare of witchcraft network, scatter, in Jesus' name

Powers praying satanic prayers against me fall down and die, in Jesus' name

Every witchcraft mirror, monitoring my life, catch fire, in Jesus' name

Wicked power swallowing the result of my prayers fall down and die, in Jesus' name

Satanic umbrella preventing heavenly blessing from reaching me, die, in Jesus' name

Arrow of confusion, fired against my brain, catch fire, in Jesus' name

Satanic garment of demotion, Holy Ghost fire consume it, in Jesus' name

Anything done against me under satanic anointing, expire, in Jesus' name

Owner of evil load, appear and carry your loads, in Jesus' name

Strange powers contending and protesting against my breakthroughs, catch fire, in Jesus' name

The poison of darkness in my root, come out now, in Jesus' name

Evil dedication that has stolen from, return what you stole from me, in Jesus' name

Witchcraft padlock, caging me, break to pieces, in Jesus' name

Witchcraft pot of bewitchment, break to pieces, in Jesus' name

Every instrument of manipulation of my star, wither, in Jesus' name

Every door opened to the enemy to attack me, close, in Jesus' name

Blood of Jesus purge my foundation from all satanic pollution, in Jesus' name

Poison of serpent and scorpion, come out of my body, in Jesus' name

The blood of Jesus purge my system of all satanic contamination, in Jesus' name

PULLING DOWN SATANIC STRONGHOLD MILITATING AGAINST YOU

Every dark stronghold wagging war against me, I pull you down, in Jesus' name

Finger of God unseat the strongman assigned against my life, in Jesus' name

Angel of God, invade every dark coven assigned against me, in Jesus' name

I cut off my body soul and spirit from every ancestral hold, in Jesus' name

Anointing of all round recovery, fall upon me, in Jesus' name

Every demonic court in procession against me, scatter, in Jesus' name

Every il decision taken against in the dark, scatter, in Jesus' name

O God, let all oppressor oppress themselves to death

I reject demonic limitation of my life and destiny, in Jesus' name

The strongman from both sides of my families. Destroy yourselves, in Jesus' name

Every spirit of Herod that wants to use me as sacrifice, die, in Jesus' name

I bind the spirit of poverty, loose your hold upon my life, in Jesus' name

O God arise and subdue my enemy under me, in Jesus' name

Let the blood of Jesus speak woe to every weapon that enemy is using against me, in Jesus' name

Blood of Jesus kill every spirit of infirmity in my body, in Jesus' name

I curse the root of the work of darkness in my life in Jesus' name

Evil bird flying for my sake, I shoot you down, in Jesus' name

O God by your prayer possibility power, give me the neck of my enemy, in Jesus' name

The negative effect of idol worship of my father, be nullified, in Jesus' name

Satanic dreams that triggers oppression, die, in Jesus' name

Deposit of spiritual spouse, dry up, in Jesus' name

Plantation of demon in the dream, be evacuated, in Jesus' name

Holy Ghost visit my life with your burning fire, in Jesus' name

Dream criminals visiting me at, what are looking for, die, in Jesus' name

Every evil family pattern of marital distress, die, in Jesus' name

No more frustration, no more satanic embargo, in Jesus' name

Power making life difficult for me, die, in Jesus' name

O God arise and let everything you have made promote me, in Jesus' name

Every good thing I lay my hands upon shall prosper, in Jesus' name

Thou power of stagnancy, break and release me, in Jesus' name

Any evil pattern of laziness sponsoring fear and wastage in my life, break, in the name of Jesus.

My life, refuse to co-operate with the spirit of laziness, in the name of Jesus.

I break free and lose myself from the grip and control of family idol spirit in the name of Jesus.

Every problem in my life promoted by idol worship, die in the name of Jesus

O Lord, deliver me from every evil pattern, emanating from evil family idol, in the name of Jesus.

Every arrow of mental disorder, fired into my brain, go back to your sender, in the name of Jesus.

Every evil computer system against my life in the demonic world, shatter to pieces, in the name of Jesus.

Any evil pot cooking my destiny, break by fire, in the name of Jesus.

Evil pattern of horrible dreams in my life, break by fire, in the name of Jesus.

Let every evil pattern of satanic discipline in my life be terminated, in the name of Jesus.

A CRY OF SOLUTION TO DIFFICULT PROBLEMS

O God arise and favor on every side, in Jesus' name

Ancient robber stealing from, give me back what you stole from me, in Jesus' name

O God arise and anchor my destiny to profitable success, in Jesus' name

O God arise and soak my life in the anointing of success, in Jesus' name

O God arise and increase my speed, in Jesus' name

Dark powers in my foundation frustrate my efforts, die, in Jesus' name

Devoured, you shall not devour me, in Jesus' name

Evil chains of stagnancy, break and let me go, in Jesus' name

Astral projection of darkness into my dream life, expire, in Jesus' name

Dark plantation assigned to cage my health, die, in Jesus' name

I shall prevail over all my enemies, in Jesus' name

O God arise and make a way for me where there is no way, in Jesus' name

I withdraw my destiny from the control of domestic witchcraft, in Jesus' name

Contrary voice speaking against me, be silenced, in Jesus' name

Satanic bank keeping my money, release it now, in Jesus' name

Wicked spirits that promote satanic dreams, die, in Jesus' name

Anyone sacrificing the blood animal to cage me, expire, in Jesus' name

Any hiring evil prophet against me, expire, in Jesus' name

I pursue, I over take and I recover all, in Jesus' name

Rain of abundant blessings, soak my life, in Jesus' name

Anointing to succeed where others failed, fall upon m, in Jesus' name

I fire back arrow of failure fired against me, in Jesus' name

Anyone cursing my destiny in the dark, be silenced, in Jesus' name

The plan of the wicked to make me labor in vain, fail, in Jesus' name

The battle of life shall not consume me, in Jesus' name

Dark charm buried for my sake, expire, in Jesus' name

Anti promotion dreams, die, in Jesus' name

My destiny shall not be cover in shame and reproach, in Jesus' name

The spirit of almost there working against me, die, in Jesus' name

I prophesy success, peace and progress into my life, in Jesus' name

DELIVERANCE FROM STUBBORN FOUNDATIONAL BONDAGE

I bind the strongman over my life and destiny, in Jesus' name

Demonic instruction given to Mother Earth to harm me, expire, in Jesus' name

The horn of darkness assigned against me, wither, in Jesus' name

The padlock of household wickedness, break to pieces, in Jesus' name

Witchcraft aggression against my star, scatter, in Jesus' name

Garment of shame, catch fire, in Jesus' name

O God arise and rend the heaven for my sake, in Jesus' name

Spell of darkness limiting me, break, to pieces, in Jesus' name

I arrest, paralyze and destroy serpent of delay, assigned against me, in Jesus' name

Marine cage break and release me, in Jesus' name

The chain of glory killer, break, in Jesus' name

The enemy of my open heaven, expire, in Jesus' name

Power asking me to appear where I am not supposed to appear, die, in Jesus' name

Blessing of the Lord without sorrow explode in my life, in Jesus' name

O God arise and glorify yourself in my life, in Jesus' name

I break the authority of demon over my life, in Jesus' name

Every crystal ball of darkness, catch fire, in Jesus' name

Battle that is older than me and stronger than me, die, in Jesus' name

Every witchcraft basket caging my wealth, catch fire, in Jesus' name

Evil pilot of satanic aircraft against me crash land, in Jesus' name

My talent be connected to favor permanently, in Jesus' name

Witchcraft cauldron working against me, catch fire, in Jesus'

Every bewitchment on my certificate, be removed, in Jesus' name

Evil pot cooking my flesh, catch fire, in Jesus' name

Satanic trade by barter, expire, in Jesus' name

Witchcraft handwriting of failure and defeat in my life, dry up, in Jesus' name

Spirit of divination assigned against my future, expire, in Jesus' name

My life shall harbor any seed of darkness, in Jesus' name

My foundation, you shall not stop my rising, in Jesus' name

O God arise and advance my life by fire, in Jesus' name.

BREAKING THE BACKBONE OF DOMESTIC WITCHCRAFT

I break the backbone of stubborn domestic witchcraft powers assigned against me

Witchcraft radar and mirror of darkness assigned against me, catch fire,

Powers that suck blood, my life is not your candidate, in Jesus' name

Witchcraft animal programmed against me die, in Jesus' name

Holy Ghost break the cord of darkness drag to wrong location, in Jesus' name

Arrow of spiritual and physical paralysis fire at me, backfire, in Jesus' name

Ancestral cage holding my destiny, break, in Jesus' name

Battle that sponsors gradual loss of good things, die, in Jesus' name

The investment of household witchcraft on my life and destiny, catch fire, in Jesus' name

Thou power of sweating without results, die, in Jesus' name

Evil dedication working against me, break, in Jesus' name

Counterfeit garment of stagnancy, catch fire, in Jesus' name

Eaters of flesh and drinker of blood, my life is not your candidate, die, in Jesus' name

Poverty yokes break from my neck, in Jesus' name

Padlock of darkness holding my breakthrough, catch fire, in Jesus' name

Every bound of sickness holding my favor, break, in Jesus' name

Poison of marine come out of my body, in Jesus' name

Witchcraft instrument of manipulation assigned against m, catch fire, in Jesus' name

The spell of thou shall not excel on my life, break, in Jesus' name

Thunder fire of God destroy every satanic cage around me, in Jesus' name

Witchcraft mirror monitoring, break to pieces, in Jesus' name

O God arise and the yoke of poverty in my life, die, in Jesus' name

Mark of possibility of God, appear in my life, in Jesus' name

My life shall not harbor the anointing of defeat, in Jesus' name

Divine opportunity beyond explanation manifest in my life by fire, in Jesus' name

Father Lord, let your angels of blessing locate today, in Jesus' name

My glory shall not be exchanged, in Jesus' name

Family strongman sponsoring poverty and failure in my life, die, in Jesus' name

Rain of divine favor, fall upon me, in Jesus' name

O God arise and turn my sorrow to joy, in this prayer, in Jesus' name

DELIVERANCE FROM EVIL FAMILY ALTARS

Every witchcraft food I have eaten that is being problems into my life, come out and die, in Jesus' name

Powers, feeding me at night with poison, wither and expire, in Jesus' name

Conspiracy of death, I am not candidate, expire and die, in Jesus' name

The hands of Jehovah repair every damage done to me by night criminals, in Jesus' name

Power of the night, calling me to appear where I am not supposed to appear, die, in Jesus' name

Powers using the hours of the night to afflict me, die, in Jesus' name

Courts of wicked elders accusing me for what I did not do, die, in Jesus' name

Powers, using my calendar date, to project disaster for me wither and die, in Jesus' name

Rain of affliction and storm of trouble, my life rejects you, dry up, in Jesus' name

Powers holding evil prayer meeting against me at night, scatter, in Jesus' name

The powers opening prison door asking me to enter, I push into your prison, in Jesus' name good

O God arise and convert my failure to success and my defeat to victory, in Jesus' name

I wage war against failure and poverty by the power in the blood of Jesus, in Jesus' name

Powers digging grave for my glory I bury you inside your grave, in Jesus' name

Powers assigned to suffocate my health and my peace, I bind you, die, in Jesus' name

O God arise and deliver me from problems I brought into my life without knowing, in Jesus' name

Winds of sorrow, I command you to dry up, in Jesus' name

Mark and label if domestic witchcraft, dry up from my body, in Jesus' name

Evil pattern of my father's following me where ever I go, die, in Jesus' name

Assembly of glory hunters assigned against me, wither and scatter, in Jesus' name

Every gadget that is installed to cage me catch fire

Destiny killer fashioned against me, kill yourself, in Jesus' name

Agenda of blood polluters die, in Jesus' name

Let every device that expected to work against me catch fire, in Jesus' name

Witchcraft power manipulating my marriage, die, in Jesus' name

The cage of darkness fashioned against me, catch fire

The padlock assigned to hold me down, break to pieces, in Jesus' name

Every arrow of delay fired at me from the dream, return back to your sender

I remove the hands of witches and wizards from the affairs of my life, in Jesus' name

I use the power in the blood of Jesus to break every yoke that says I shall not amount to anything, in Jesus' name

DELIVERANCE FROM THE GRIP OF HOUSE HOLD WICKEDNESS

I cancel every conscious and unconscious marriage agreement with any dark power, in the name of Jesus

Every of evil smell sprayed on me at night be roasted, by fire, in Jesus' name

Every pollution in the dream that scare helper away during the day burn to ashes, in Jesus' name

Blood of Jesus pass through my entire system and flush out evil smell, in Jesus' name

Holy Ghost let your burning fire burn off inherited evil smell, in Jesus' name

Every witchcraft injection to poison my spirit man, clear away, by the blood of Jesus, in Jesus' name

I break and release myself every smell of death, in Jesus' name

Thou witchcraft perfume of gradual decaying, die, in Jesus' name

Every witchcraft perfume of rejection, blood of Jesus, clear it away from me, in Jesus' name

Witchcraft arrow drying the oil of favor from my head, come out and die, in Jesus' name

Strange personality following me anywhere I go, receive arrow of death, in Jesus' name

I release myself from the pollution emanating from the waters, in Jesus' name

Witchcraft urinating on my project of prosperity fall down and die, in Jesus' name

Progress and joy terminating evil seed in my life, be uprooted by fire, in Jesus' name

Every miracle buried seed in my life, catch fire, in Jesus' name

Witchcraft ointment on my fore head dry up, in Jesus' name

Every setback promoting dream, in my life, burn to ashes, in Jesus' name

Masquerade of ancestral spirit chasing me at night die, in Jesus' name

Witchcraft market where the buying and selling of my star is taking place, close down and burn to ashes, in Jesus' name

Every witchcraft monitoring object assigned to watch nigh and be destroyed, in Jesus' name

The serpent carrying the poison of death assigned against poison yourself and die, in Jesus' name

The power that wants me to exist without living, die, in Jesus' name

The power that wants to convert my day to night, die, in Jesus' name

Anyone who vowed that he or she would rather die than see me succeed, expire, in Jesus' name

My picture on any evil altar be withdrawn by fire, in Jesus' name

Thou witchcraft power, expanding and multiplying my problems, die, in Jesus' name

Every witchcraft mark disappear from my body now, in Jesus' name

The tongue loaded with enchantment, speaking against me, be silenced, in Jesus' name

I overthrow the disappears food from the dining table of the enemy, in Jesus' name

Every enchantment programmed into the air to catch, catch your owner, in Jesus' name

BREAKING THE YOKE OF FAMILIAR SPIRITS AND MARINE SPIRITS

Witchcraft burial done against me and my star, expire, in Jesus' name

O God arise and promote me, in the midst of those says, I am finished, in Jesus' name

Every pattern of disgrace assigned to make a laughing stock, catch fire, in Jesus' name

Judas of the night, assigned to hand me over for slaughter, b destroyed, in Jesus' name

Powers, feeding me at night with poison, wither and expire, in Jesus' name

Conspiracy of death, I am not candidate, expire and die, in Jesus' name

The hands of Jehovah repair every damage done to me by night criminals, in Jesus' name

Power of the night, calling me to appear where I am not supposed to appear, die, in Jesus' name

Powers using the hours of the night to afflict me, die, in Jesus' name

Courts of wicked elders accusing me for what I did not do, die, in Jesus' name

Powers, using my calendar date, to project disaster for me wither and die, in Jesus' name

Rain of affliction and storm of trouble, my life rejects you, dry up, in Jesus' name

Powers holding evil prayer meeting against me at night, scatter, in Jesus' name

The powers opening prison door asking me to enter, I push into your prison, in Jesus' name good

O God arise and convert my failure to success and my defeat to victory, in Jesus' name

I wage war against failure and poverty by the power in the blood of Jesus, in Jesus' name

Powers digging grave for my glory I bury you inside your grave, in Jesus' name

Powers assigned to suffocate my health and my peace, I bind you, die, in Jesus' name

O God arise and deliver me from problems I brought into my life without knowing, in Jesus' name

Arrow of pollution fire at me through dreams go back to your sender

I confess the sin that opened the door for the enemy to succeed, in Jesus' name

Witchcraft embargo break upon life, in Jesus' name

Rope of darkness tying me down for mockery, catch fire, in Jesus' name

Poison of slow death in my body, dry up, in Jesus' name

I cough out of my body, satanic substance I have eaten that cause sickness, in Jesus' name

Poison of marine witchcraft, come out of my body, in Jesus' name

Evil arrow in the dream that manifested in real life, come out of my body, in Jesus' name

Blood of Jesus, push out of my system food eaten from the table of the enemy, in Jesus' name

Arrow of witchcraft that convert the head to tail, die, in Jesus' name

Every unconscious 'yes' where I should have said 'no' in dream that is affecting me, be nullified, in Jesus' name

DELIVERANCE FROM BONDAGE OF POLYGAMY

Owner of evil loads, appear and carry your loads, in Jesus' name

Witchcraft cover preventing good to locate me catch fire, in Jesus' name

Witchcraft arrow that intelligent to become dull go back to your senders, in Jesus' name

My life disobedience satanic command issue against me, on any wicked altar, in Jesus' name

O God arise and let the wicked be swallowed by the evil they have devised against me, in Jesus' name

Foundational strongman assigned to cripple my elevation be crushed, in the name of Jesus

The serpent and scorpion of death assigned against me, die, in Jesus' name

My star and my glory rejects witchcraft bewitchment, in the name of Jesus

Every resistance to my advancement and acceleration, be dashed to pieces, in Jesus' name

Wedding rings and clothes of marine burn to ashes, in Jesus' name

Holy Ghost fire burn the properties of the marine in my custody, in Jesus' name

Blood of Jesus separate from every marine dedication working against me, in Jesus' name

Holy Ghost fire consume the certificate of marriage with any marine agent with your fire, in Jesus' name

O Lord repair any damage done to my life by any marine now, in Jesus' name

Every connection or covenant I have with any idol, break, in Jesus' name

From henceforth let no marine spirit harass me, in Jesus' name

I overthrow the seat of the marine, working against, catch fire, in Jesus' name

This year the world will know I am serving a living God, in Jesus' name

O Lord thou art a shield for me and the lifter of my head, O God arise and lift my head, in Jesus' name

My positive change I have been waiting for, manifest by fire, in Jesus' name

This year I shall encounter any embarrassment, shame, and disgrace, in Jesus' name

Every work of the enemy in my life, come to an end, in Jesus' name

Evil voice speaking to counter my breakthroughs, be silenced, in Jesus' name

This year I reject insult and I claim undeniable result, in Jesus' name

Barriers erected against my lifting, clear away by fire, in Jesus' name

Demonic campaigns against my celebration, fail, in Jesus' name

By the finger of God, let all my obstacles give way to my miracles, in Jesus' name

Ruler of darkness hijacking and diverting what belongs to me, die, in Jesus' name

Any charm or fetish powers assigned against me, expire, in Jesus' name

The voice of accusations before my helpers, you shall speak no more, in Jesus' name

DELIVERANCE FROM PLACENTAL BONDAGE

Problems assigned to grow up with me till old age, die, in Jesus' name

Where ever the good things I have been expecting is tied down, be released, in Jesus' name

Satanic womb that has swallowed my blessings, vomit it by fire, in Jesus' name

I connect to 24-hour breakthroughs by the power in the blood of Jesus, in Jesus' name

Power polluting my blood, you're a liar; die in the name of Jesus!

Every demonic access to my blood, expire in the name of Jesus!

Ancestral documents and records in my blood, catch fire in the name of Jesus!

O God arise, infuse spiritual vitamins to my blood for prayer energy in the name of Jesus!

All negative materials circulating in my blood stream, die in the name of Jesus!

Holy Ghost fire, enter into my bloodstream and cleanse my bloodstream in the name of Jesus!

Blood of Jesus, be transfused into my blood system in the name of Jesus!

Any evil blood that mingled with my blood, be drained out in the name of Jesus!

Any strange hand that has touched my blood, be evacuated now in the name of Jesus!

O God arise, pump the blood of Jesus into my bloodstream in the name of Jesus!

Strangers in my blood, I'm not your candidate; get out in the name of Jesus!

Holy Ghost, immunize my blood against spiritual poisons in the name of Jesus!

I withdraw my blood and any part of my body from any evil alter in the name of Jesus!

Evil voices summoning my blood, shut up and die in the name of Jesus!

Blood of Jesus, flush out every evil material in my blood in the name of Jesus!

My blood, reject every witchcraft poison in the name of Jesus!

Sword of deliverance from heaven, touch my blood now in the name of Jesus!

Any part of my blood, swallowed by drinkers of blood; vomit them now in the name of Jesus!

My spirit, soul and body reject evil plantation, in Jesus' name

Holy Ghost make my life conducive for your presence, in Jesus' name

Demon shall not use my body as their evil habitation, in Jesus' name

Death and destruction shall not feed on my body, in Jesus' name

Every blood speaking against my blood line, shut up and die, in Jesus' name

Every unconscious witchcraft altar, ministering against me, catch fire, in Jesus' name

Arrow of affliction fired against me, loose your hold, in Jesus' name

Where is the Lord God of Elijah, I tear down the altar of magician hired against me, in Jesus' name

VIOLENT PRAYERS AGAINST UNREPENTANT HOUSEHOLD WICKEDNESS AND PURSUERS

Satanic dedication that speaks against my glory, be silenced, in Jesus' name

Every good thing houses I have lived in the past have stolen from me, I take it back, in Jesus' name

I vomit every dark food, I have eaten from the table of the enemy, in Jesus' name

Let every stubborn pursuer of my life turn back from me, in Jesus' name

My life, you shall not cooperate with evil designer, in Jesus' name

Chain of oppression, limiting me, break, in Jesus' name

Holy Ghost package me for Miracles, signs and wonders, in Jesus' name

O Lord, according the greatness of your power, manifest yourself in my life, in Jesus' name

Any problems in my life programmed to die with me, you are liar, die, in Jesus' name

Any carried over battle that is attacking me back and front, expire by the blood of Jesus

Every ancient covenant limiting my joy, be destroy to the root, in Jesus' name

I command darkness to cover the enemies that are after my soul, in Jesus' name

Wicked pursuers of my destiny, become deaf and dumped and let confusion envelope suddenly, in Jesus' name

Powers that have vowed to cover me with shame, be covered with shame, in Jesus' name

All those that wants to destroy me, I command you to face yourselves and destroy yourselves, in Jesus' name

Every altar sponsoring my enemy against me, catch fire and be roasted, in Jesus' name

By the authority of the blood of Jesus, my life shall be cut short at the prime of my life, my light shall become dark in the daylight, in Jesus' name

The angels that killed Herod, arise and locate where evil people are gathered and kill them, in Jesus' name

Arrow fired to weaken my prayer life, backfire, in Jesus' name

Strongman shadow following me anywhere I go to steal from me, die suddenly, in Jesus' name

Any bad things currently happened in my life cease from today, in Jesus' name

Every word spoken to render my glory redundant, be reversed, in Jesus' name

Every altar erected against me that is behind epileptic progress, catch fire, in Jesus' name

Angels of my arise and activate ceaseless favor in my life, in Jesus' name

Every good thing in my line that are locked up in any witchcraft pot, be released, in Jesus' name

Holy fire bomb, explode on the face of my stubborn enemies and destroy them, in Jesus' name

Wild wind of the Lord, arise and pull down every altar erected against me, in Jesus' name

The stubborn root of my problem, dry up, in Jesus' name

Problems of my life, your time is over, carry yourself back to where you came from, in Jesus' name

Evil load and satanic deposits, come out of your hiding place, in Jesus' name

LADEJOLA ABIODUN

PRAYERS TO DESTROY OPPRESSION AND BONDAGE

Any evil pattern of laziness sponsoring fear and wastage in my life, break, in the name of Jesus.

My life, refuse to co-operate with the spirit of laziness, in the name of Jesus.

I break free and lose myself from the grip and control of family idol spirit in the name of Jesus.

Every problem in my life promoted by idol worship, die in the name of Jesus

O Lord, deliver me from every evil pattern, emanating from evil family idol, in the name of Jesus.

Every arrow of mental disorder, fired into my brain, go back to your sender, in the name of Jesus.

Every evil computer system against my life in the demonic world, shatter to pieces, in the name of Jesus.

Any evil pot cooking my destiny, break by fire, in the name of Jesus.

Evil pattern of horrible dreams in my life, break by fire, in the name of Jesus.

Let every evil pattern of satanic discipline in my life be terminated, in the name of Jesus

Witchcraft poison hiding in any part of my life, I challenge with fire, come out of your hiding, in Jesus' name

I retrieve my favor from where the enemy is hiding it, in Jesus' name

Battles with agenda to finish me, finish yourself, in Jesus' name

I receive power of the Holy Ghost to put my enemy under my feet permanently, in Jesus' name

Domestic witches and wizard fueling my problems, receive judgement of death, in Jesus' name

Any group of persons that have entered into covenant to destroy me, destroy yourselves, in Jesus' name

Anyone using my picture to fight or attack me, die on your evil altar, in Jesus' name

Mid night masquerade that are saying my testimonies will not manifest, die, in Jesus' name

Every padlock employed to trouble my health, break to pieces, in Jesus' name

Powers and forces of darkness making it difficult for me to obtain favor and good will run mad and die, in Jesus' name

Powers forcing evil garments on me in the spirit, your end has come, die, in Jesus' name

Covenant of suffering break over the works of my hands, in Jesus' name

Covenant of suffering that is diverting my favor to another place, break, in Jesus' name

I declare war against poverty, sickness and ignorance, in Jesus' name

Every damage done to my destiny before now, be repaired, by the power, in the Blood of Jesus

O Lord anoint my eyes to see opportunities where others see problem, in Jesus' name

Powers of the grave that is contending for my breakthroughs, die, in Jesus' name

Satan, strongman, ancestral spirit, remove your hands from my glory, in Jesus' name

Anointing to excel and prosper beyond this level fall upon me, in Jesus' name

All my imprisoned and buried potentials what are you waiting for, be released and manifest, in Jesus' name

Every deeply rooted problem in my life, come out with all your root, in Jesus' name

I refuse to live as slave, and I refuse to live a floating destiny, in Jesus' name

Garment of darkness, my neck and my body are not your candidate, in Jesus' name

O God arise, uproot evil seed that is not planted by you from my life, In Jesus' name

Holy Ghost fire set me free from any strong room of darkness, where I am detained, in Jesus' name

Garment of sickness and infinity my body rejects you, catch fire, in Jesus' name

Every poison hiding in my blood, come out now, in Jesus' name

LADEJOLA ABIODUN

PRAYERS OF DELIVERANCE FROM LIMITATION AND STAGNATION

Any evil pattern of laziness sponsoring fear and wastage in my life, break, in the name of Jesus.

My life, refuse to co-operate with the spirit of laziness, in the name of Jesus.

I break free and lose myself from the grip and control of family idol spirit in the name of Jesus.

Every problem in my life promoted by idol worship, die in the name of Jesus

O Lord, deliver me from every evil pattern, emanating from evil family idol, in the name of Jesus.

Every arrow of mental disorder, fired into my brain, go back to your sender, in the name of Jesus.

Every evil computer system against my life in the demonic world, shatter to pieces, in the name of Jesus.

Any evil pot cooking my destiny, break by fire, in the name of Jesus.

Evil pattern of horrible dreams in my life, break by fire, in the name of Jesus.

Let every evil pattern of satanic discipline in my life be terminated, in the name of Jesus.

The foundational strongman assigned to cripple my elevation, fall down and die, in Jesus' name

O God arise let the wicked be swallowed by the evil they have imagined against me, in Jesus' name

Every door of progress shut against me, open, in Jesus' name

Every resistance to my divine acceleration and promotion, be dashed to pieces, in Jesus' name

Thou power of emptier and waster assigned against me, be destroyed, in Jesus' name

Internal and external devices of domestic witchcraft blocking the rising of my star, burn to ashes, in Jesus' name

Serpent and scorpion of failure at the edge of success, die, in Jesus' name

No wickedness shall prevail against me, in Jesus' name

My star and glory rejects bewitchment, in Jesus' name

Hamman diverting my breakthrough, wither, in Jesus' name

Witchcraft padlock that holds destiny down in the place of frustration, die, in Jesus' name

Association of wicked elders on assignment against my life, scatter, in Jesus' name

Evil speaking against my success, wither, in Jesus' name

O God by your power, bring me out of every valley of working without results, die, in Jesus' name

Invisible chains of environmental witchcraft in my hands, break, in Jesus' name

Satanic legislation working against me, be nullified, in Jesus' name

The concluded work of darkness against my prosperity, scatter, in Jesus' name

Ancestral witchcraft embargo, break, in Jesus' name

Wind of positive change blow in my favor, in Jesus' name

The wickedness of the wicked, expire today, in Jesus' name

Every satanic set up to frustrate me, be dismantled, in Jesus' name

Thou spirit of almost there but never there, assigned against me, die, in Jesus' name

LADEJOLA ABIODUN

BOOKS BY PASTOR LADEJOLA ABIODUN

Commanding Supernatural Blessings

Deliverance from Captivity

Provoke Your Deliverance

Our God Is a Big God

Power to Defeat Satanic Agents

Power to Move from Poverty to Prosperity

Eagle Believer

O Lord, I Need a Miracle

A Successful Home

The Mystery of Angelic Intervention

The Mystery of Power

When Your Battle Is from Home

The Lost Signs

The Power of Prophetic Destiny

Power to Make Maximum Impact

Power Against Stubborn Death

I Reject Satanic Embarrassment

Power Against Environmental Limitation

Your Season of Promotion

No More Dryness

Who Is to Be Blamed?

War Against Environmental Poverty

The Mystery of Divine Favor

Power to Trouble Your Trouble

Converting Your Pain to Gain

Dealing with Programmed Affliction

Don't Play Games with God

Dealing with Witchcraft Barriers

Helps for Your Marriage

I Shall Get to the Top

O Lord, Remember Me

Prayer for Extraordinary Achievement

The Mystery of Expectation

The God of Possibility

Winning War Against Poverty

No More Delay

The Lord Is a Man of War

When the Eagle Is Caged

The Mystery of Generational Battle

Breaking the Chains of Darkness

Promoted by Favor

Provoking Divine Intervention

I Need Fresh Fire

Connecting to Miracles, Signs & Wonders

The Incomparable God

Dealing With Stubborn Bondage

Made in the USA
Columbia, SC
12 May 2024

35565034R00104